Dissolving the Masks

An Artist's Tour of the Unconscious

Jean Ford

Dissolving the Masks © 2021 Jean Ford

All rights reserved. No part of this book may be reproduced in any form or by any electronic or mechanical means, including information storage and retrieval systems, without permission in writing from the author, except for the inclusion of brief quotations in a review.

Book designer: Naomi C. Rose
Cover art: Jean Ford
Typeface: Garamond

With thanks to Bruce H. Lipton, PhD, for permission to quote from his interviews about The Biology of Belief. www.brucelipton.com

This personal story is for information purposes only, and is not intended to serve as an alternative to any therapy. Readers with significant challenges are encouraged to seek the guidance of professionals. Readers' use of the material is at their own discretion, and they are responsible for their own experiences.

ISBN 978-0-9836333-2-7

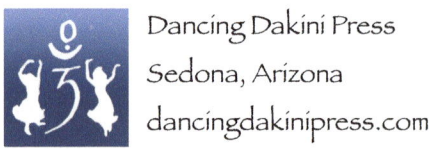

Dancing Dakini Press
Sedona, Arizona
dancingdakinipress.com

Dedication

To Mike, who set forth on his quest alone,
where there was no path.
The vision he acquired still lights his path
and the lives of those who walk with him
on this journey.

Love Is The Fulfillment

1 Corinthians 13:1-8 11-13

Though I speak with the tongues of men and of angels, and have not love, I am become as sounding brass, or a tinkling cymbal.

And though I have the gift of prophecy, and understand all mysteries, and all knowledge; and though I have all faith, so that I could remove mountains, and have not love, I am nothing.

And though I bestow all my goods to feed the poor, and though I give my body to be burned, and have not love, it profiteth me nothing.

Love suffereth long, and is kind; love envieth not; love vaunteth not itself, is not puffed up,

Doth not behave itself unseemly, seeketh not her own, is not easily provoked, thinketh no evil;

Rejoiceth not in iniquity, but rejoiceth in the truth;

Beareth all things, believeth all things, hopeth all things, endureth all things.

Love never faileth: but whether there be prophecies, they shall fail; whether there be tongues, they shall cease; whether there be knowledge, it shall vanish away.

For we know in part, and we prophesy in part.

But when that which is perfect is come, then that which is in part shall be done away.

When I was a child, I spake as a child, I understood as a child, I thought as a child: but when I became a man, I put away childish things.

For now we see through a glass, darkly; but then face to face: now I know in part; but then shall I know even as also I am known.

And now abideth faith, hope, love, these three; but the greatest of these is love.

Introduction

❖ The Origins of This Book

If you are like me, you too suffered multiple traumas before the age of three from people who were crippled in their own humanness. For me, the world did not make sense. I chose to survive, so I developed many coping skills, which served me for many years. I grew up with no place for my feelings – rage, sadness, grief, fear, and anxiety. There was an inner conviction that I was not okay.

During my journey, I learned, at ever-increasing depths, that trauma keeps fragments of a person locked in the past, fragments that stay frozen. Those subparts, frequently beneath awareness, relive the original trauma. I had to learn to be compassionate toward the child in myself who had to develop survival skills that distorted so much of my later life. Yes, I am still occasionally too nice – pleasing kept me alive. Yes, I did not develop my voice until recently – my silence and hiding kept me alive.

I went into an adult world unprepared. In hindsight, I realize I had no idea who I was except a compliant, obedient, helpful child who'd been shamed into dependency with a "good girl" mask. I still wanted to please. That is all I knew. By setting boundaries, such as saying, "No," I took my power back.

I am writing to you because very few people knew, until very late in my own life, how to work creatively with early-trauma sufferers. I worked in different therapy modes: object relations, Jungian analysis, art therapy, family constellation and others. Seldom was I confronted with what I (or a split-off frozen personality fragment created by early trauma) was doing. Instead for years, I reviewed the traumas over and over in a paradigm where my parents were abusive and there was something wrong with me, something wrong with my parents. The culture also systematically sends fear, hate, and false information into the perceptions of everyone. It operates like a program – no one escapes.

Recently, my inner journey of self-awareness reached a tipping point, after many years of effort. At a pivotal moment, I was amazed to notice that I was no longer a suffering victim but a mature, intelligent, self-aware woman. I felt impulses to bring even more light and love into this very familiar story – in my own life and in the lives of anyone I can reach by publishing these artworks. The processes described in this book are part of my own deep experience of transformation.

I did learn during the years of therapy. Some of the themes of those partial awakenings are reflected in the artwork in the next section. You might find your own themes: since this kind of art is, by definition, mostly wordless, you'll have your own reactions, your own interpretations. I'll share some of my haikus to stimulate your imagination when viewing my artwork.

One important revelation was realizing that living with intense, unresolved early traumas had set up addictions to emotional states and their associated neurochemicals. The element of chemical addiction altered my entire perception of my situation: it was the work of epigenetics specialist Bruce Lipton (*The Biology of Belief*) that brought this wholly new understanding into my life, and as he frequently says, "The moment you change your perception is the moment you rewrite the chemistry of your body." Healing accelerated when this idea took hold, and yet there was still much more to understand.

When the internalized abuse stories played over and over, they generated the same emotions and familiar neurological patterns, creating a merry-go-round I could not stop. It took years for me to stop judging myself for continuing to go around in these agonizing circles, these feedback loops.

Investigating the feedback loops required therapeutic attention. For example, I learned the difference between needs and desires: I saw that my power-seeking behaviors had risen up to protect me, to cover deep feelings of insecurity, and I could see that these polar opposites went around in a loop. I also discovered I'd been seeking relationships to fill my well of despair. Eventually, I came to understand that attempting to meet these delusional needs from inside the experience of delusional neediness would never work.

Remembering experiences of anguish was the beginning point for a richer, deeper compassion for myself and others. I also saw that contemplation of this idea was loosening the addictive grip of emotions and neurochemicals associated with victimhood. I could feel compassion for myself without the enveloping haze of guilt and fear.

When I decided to go inside to heal, I committed to a life-long process. To get below the entanglements, the chaos, it took courage and a willingness to consider that a state of consciousness beyond my normal waking state was guiding me. Eventually, this openness allowed me to consciously experience the Life Force as an intelligent, loving power. I was able to choose love. Finally I knew, at profound and transcendent levels, something that I'd intellectually understood for decades: there is a greater reality, a greater truth that dissolves the false while truth remains.

After all the ventures into distorted truth, fresh insights were possible. I learned to be honest with myself. I would no longer avoid pain: emotional, physical, and/or mental. As a result, my life opened up to deeper levels of consciousness. I learned there are no spiritual bypasses.

It might take years – times of depression, anxiety, not belonging, years of not knowing when your unique cosmic self will arise. It is part of the healing process, which might include breathwork, energy work, and movement like yoga or dance, to embody the changes. It's important to have skilled helpers in these body/mind disciplines, if you're working with severe inner distortions, since the changes can be so profound and occasionally unsettling. This is not a solo journey. When you commit to your intention to heal no matter what, it's my hope and belief that guides, mentors, and healers will arrive to support you.

I realize how fortunate I've been in that regard. If you do find capable people, each helper will bring forward parts of you that have been frozen in time and space, parts you've never consciously experienced before, bringing all your life into the present moment.

To envision the potential, you must wake up from the dream, the dream in which emotions are blocked from awareness and, on their own, flood the body/mind with feelings that have been unexpressed, unidentified, unnamed. When those feelings are at last experienced with awareness, there can be a tremendous release. There can also be chaotic instability, accompanied by changes in biochemistry, followed by joy and freedom – unforced.

The healers working with me in this unfolding process specialized in different styles of human emergence. I felt their love, their compassion at the edges of my boundary. They encouraged me to listen to my own inner teacher. The truth I needed was within and revealed itself when I was ready. I am grateful for everyone who lit up pathways into my self-awareness, without which the tipping point might never have become possible.

In preparing this book, with its visual and verbal expressions of those pathways, I experienced a sort of weaving together of several dimensions. Deep into the process, I discovered I was weaving a new fabric of multidimensional understanding for myself. This fabric had a coherence of design I'd never experienced before. It was exhilarating. The thrill deepened even more when I recognized that I was reweaving and rewiring my own neural networks, so that all aspects of my being could communicate gracefully with one another, in ever-richer mutual awareness. This kind of interdimensionality is useful for more than just personal healing: a polyphasic worldview can move us all in more creative directions.

My process began with spontaneous artwork. It is important to have some uninterrupted safe space to fully engage the process. I realize this can be difficult to attain, but it's worth the effort. In my case, the Covid-19 Pandemic ensured days, weeks, months for me to journey into the depths of my conscious and unconscious worlds. I set up a retreat space that remained consistent throughout the creation stages. A large window allowed sunlight to warm and brighten the area. I laid out pencils, erasers, colored pencils, crayons, Magic Markers, and five mixed-media sketch books. My dining room table provided a large enough surface on which to work. In the evenings, a large ginger-jar lamp lit up the space. A framed quote from the poet Hafez was always within view: "Do what most enables you to fly."

What do you think? What do you feel? I'm asking you now because being aware of your reactions to my words and pictures will provide you with insights into your inner journey. Emotions, memories, family secrets, might surface. Be gentle with yourself, find support, and with perseverance and courage the time will come when you will recognize your true nature.

❖ The Origins of the Masks

I was born in 1946. World War II was over – a time of booming prosperity and peace. Growing up with television programs like *Leave It to Beaver* numbed me into believing all was well.

The rules were simple and mostly unspoken: keep the respectable family image in place, no matter what; never ever share family secrets like incest, alcoholism, abuse, infidelity; be in church on Sundays as a family unit; get a college degree; absolutely never question or criticize your parents, teachers, the church – anyone in authority. Everything unpleasant was on lockdown in my dysfunctional family.

The hero's journey started for me when I had to acknowledge a depression that started in my thirties. While holding down a responsible job and functioning in society, weekly therapy helped uncover the well guarded secrets that formed what I eventually came to understand as a shame-based personality. I could not talk about going to therapy sessions, for fear of losing employment, losing status in the community. Still, the revelations of therapy were vital.

It was there that I remembered the trauma of being hospitalized for a month at about age three for a congenital condition that doctors advised my parents would be fatal. At that time, doctors believed it was best for parents not to visit during the stay, and so attachment under these conditions was impossible.

The issues that then surfaced over the years were staggering. As most children do, I believed everything was my fault. The shame foundation was laid. It became obvious to me that in order to birth myself I would have to take responsibility for my life as it was with no one to blame.

All of the masks formed in the earliest parts of my life helped me survive the turbulence of trauma. Decades later, dissolving all of them (including favorite ones like the butterfly, on the cover) has been a large part of my healing process. The question of "who am I" started an inquiry process that took me beyond psychological answers to a spiritual quest.

One mask in particular brought up terror: the deeply buried self-image of unworthiness (also shown on the cover). When I allowed the imagery of that mask to flow onto the page, I had to face my fear of death. I had to make a choice as many survivors do: live in fear and loathing of my shamed self, or love myself. And the process continues: being vulnerable is a choice I keep making, ever more willing to allow the masks to rise to awareness.

❖ The Origins of Hope

With years of inner work, my inner life began opening up. At the time this book goes to press, I am 74 years of age. I created this book for those who survived childhood anguish. It is the gift I bring back to the community after my own hero's journey.

I also recognize that some of the seeds for my future impulse toward self-care were planted in my early years, when I was exposed to the idea that there could be a better world. During the darkest nights of my soul, I experienced help from a transcendent, loving power that would not abandon me. It would be many, many years before I understood that that power arose from within me.

This early experience of benevolent realms beyond the material led to the creation of a daily meditation practice and the launch of worldwide explorations into religious traditions. The meditation practice was deepened in two ten-day Vipassana retreats, in Barre, Massachusetts, and 29 Palms, California.

When I was 35, I volunteered for six months in a kibbutz in northern Israel, with trips to Egypt and Greece. Later, as a Franciscan Sister, I witnessed the loving power minister to the disenfranchised living in Milwaukee's high-rise buildings, to the women in the shelters, and to those in service. My wish for readers is that you remain open to remembering such seeds of Life.

Those tiny sparks might make it possible for you to choose Life, as I did, and unlock a path to recognizing your True Nature.

Art and Haikus

spaceless and timeless

below mind entanglements

possibilities

at last letting go

no egoic solutions

threshold of new life

alone in their world

they were absorbed in themselves

they could not see me

their power complete

sacrifice my feminine

for survival's sake

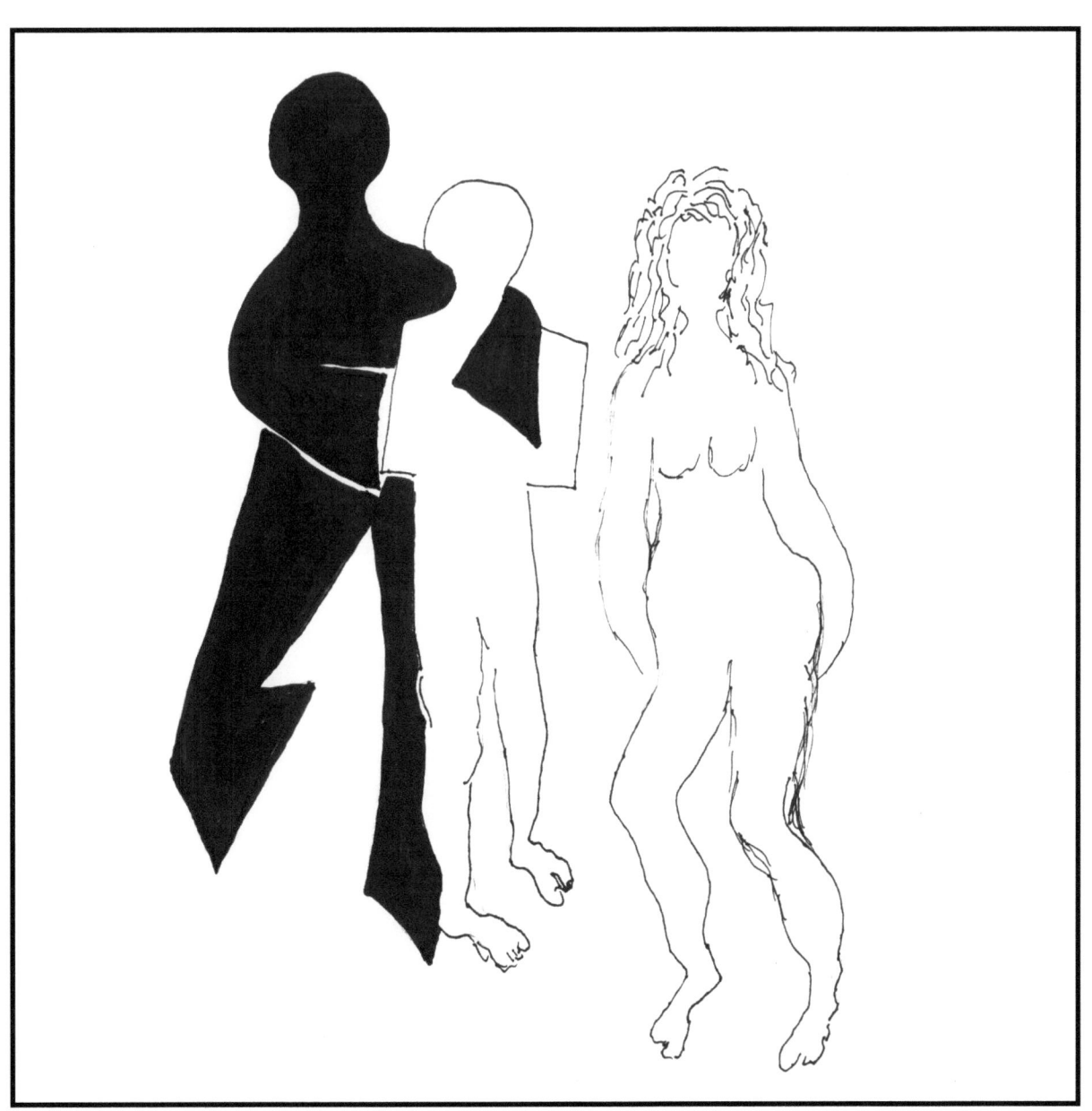

encapsulated

memory of his fury

posing as myself

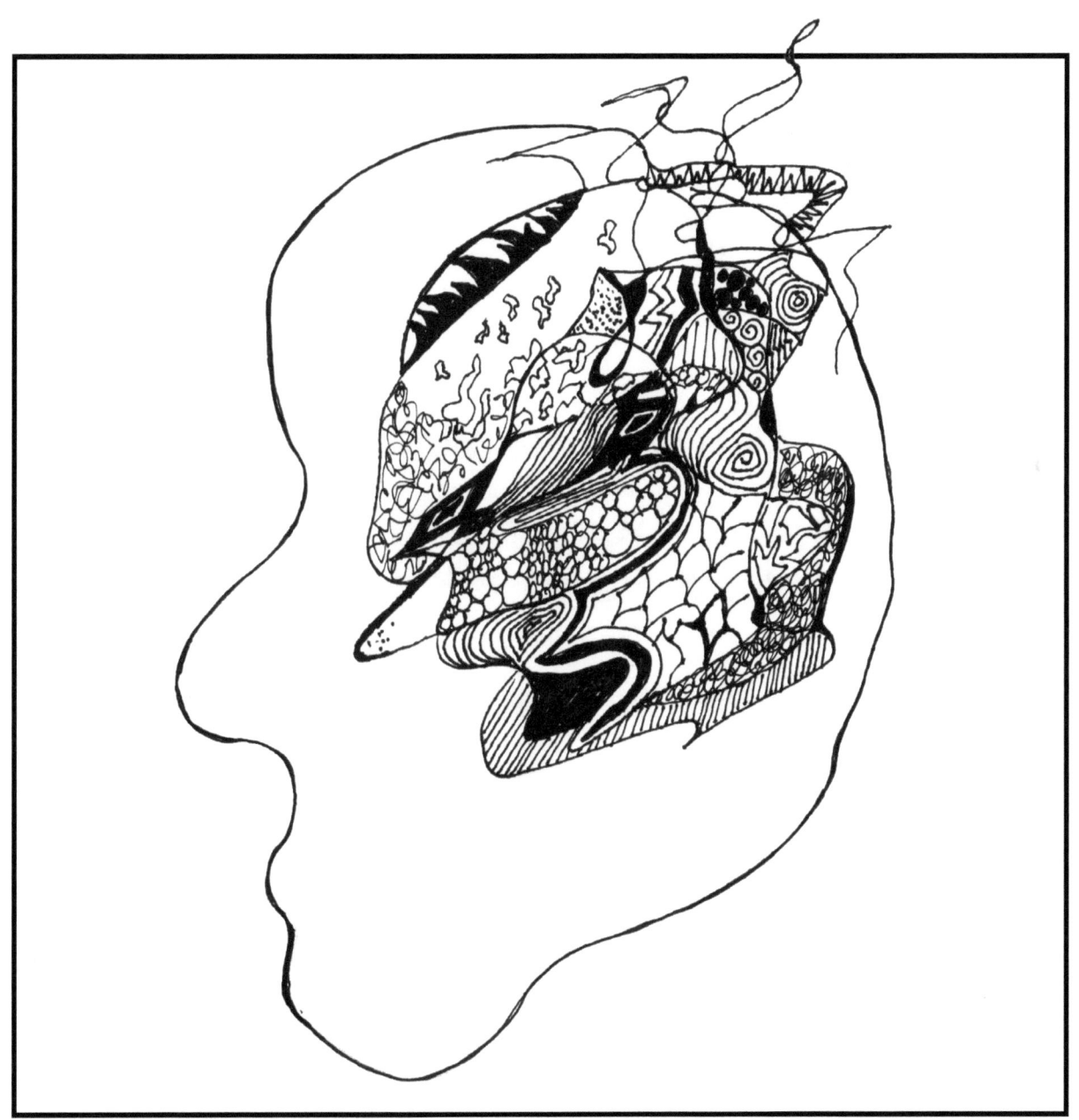

devouring mother

left me going nowhere fast

too needy to leave

severing all cords

painfully free to create

but no sense of self

seeing inner worlds

loving with no conditions

opened healing space

changing perception

the light shining in darkness

ignorance dispelled

holding the mirror

I claim all that is my self

I own the smudges

my whole life this rock

never seeing beyond it

visionless despair

slowing down – a pause

allowing what is, to be

effortless moment

awareness shifted

my struggle is our struggle

others are with me

inner turmoil stilled

safe to explore inner worlds

new life – butterfly

go into the wound

feel the pain and face the truth

arduous process

tears falling below

rage roaring up through black ice

layers on layers

trembling young soul lives

hiding under volcanos

feels life-threatening

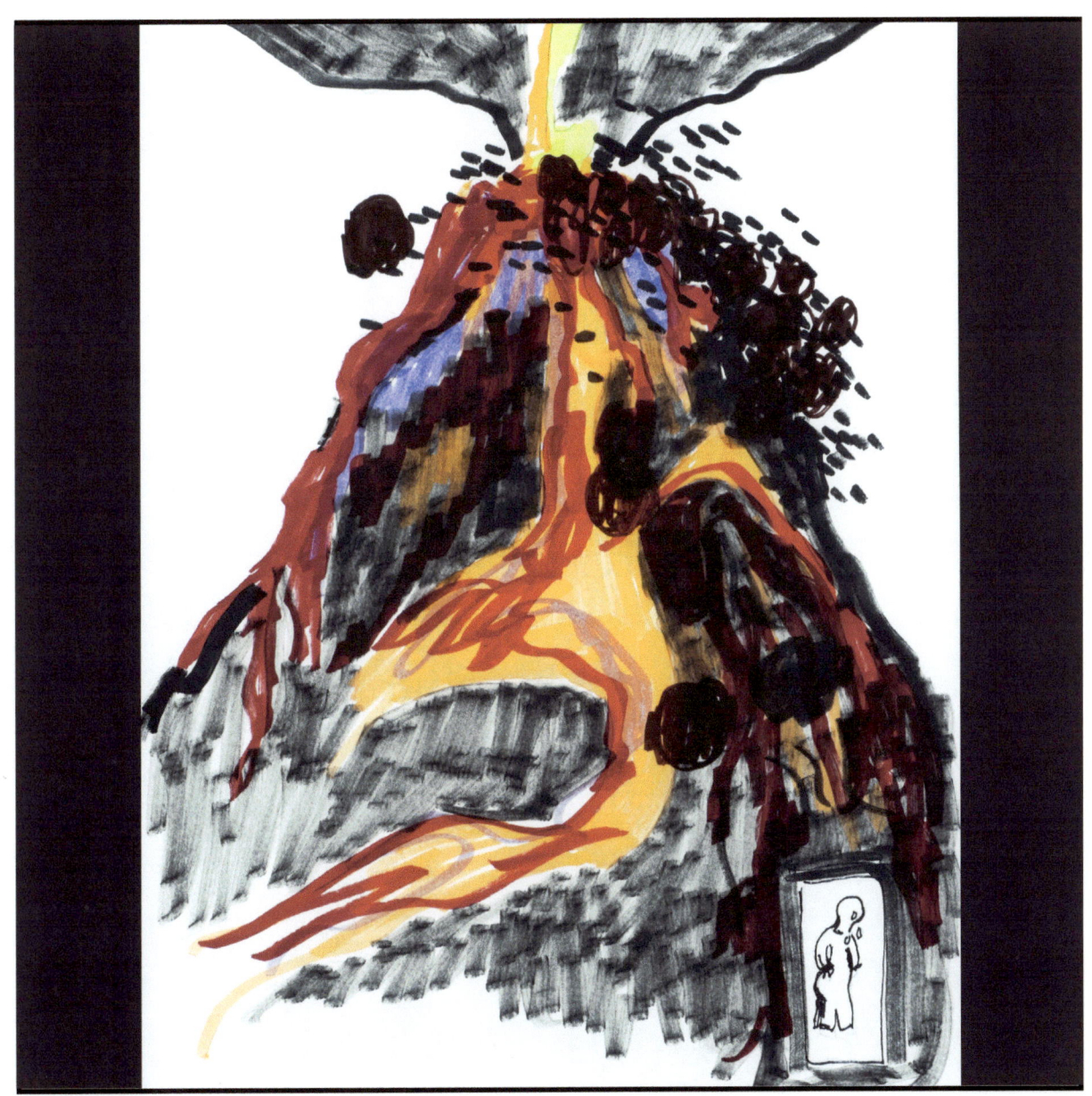

black and white thinking

inconsistent behaviors

left me terrified

void with shared edges

their narcissism shaped me

shattering my self

worthless piece of shit

world's cruel vernacular

my shame recognized

Kali dark mother

in your hand life, death, new life

held in compassion

choosing to live life

transcendent and human joined

a resurrection

feminine buried

from deep within a longing

flower emerges

dark clouds swept away

an array of brightness burst

the I bloomed open

a new world opens

each archetype caught – more I –

rising shadowed light

exploring new masks

patterns from the collective

aware not attached

seductress networker dreamer mystic seeker
sidekick princess servant addict mother
warrior alchemist prostitute dictator
coward student
pioneer
crook
nun
victim
saboteur healer
teacher
disciple
diplomat liberator lover martyr
actor fool
avenger puritan artist shaman hermit
wizard puritan child
sage judge scout magician
vampire clown

sitting quietly

an effortless awareness

of the cosmic dance

energetic waves

quantum possibilities

burgeoning intent

focusing waves pop

expressing shaped potential

living synergy

removing the mask

a shame-based identity

I think I will die

happy collisions

conscious and unconscious weave

new worlds of insight

an ever-changing

newly explored universe

contained within me

opposites resolve

no single small self is true ~

mingled radiance

ongoing process

affirms possibilities

explore no limits

Acknowledgements

I honor my mother and father for giving me life.

Kenyon Taylor offered me her full humanness in the healing container. Her compassion for THE YOUNG me helped me navigate through the most vulnerable parts of my book journey. Always empowering, she placed her confidence in my ability to heal myself. Kenyon accompanied Me back to my beginnings where the traumas of separation with my mother occured. After years of psychotherapy, I experienced a Somatic, body based therapy. The difference was I experienced in my body that I had survived. This allowed my brain to calm down enough to GET PRESENT AND TO reach the depths of my inner journey.

Naomi Rose recognized the possibility of a book as I shared some of the art pouring out of my unconscious. She held heart space for me when being vulnerable was too demanding. Naomi shared her belief that we go through these experiences not just for ourselves but to help others.

I am deeply appreciative to authors who guided my inner journey with their psychological/spiritual wisdom and insights: Bert Hellinger, A H Almass, Rollo May, Ken Wilbur, Sri Nisargadatta Maharaj.

About the Author

The art in this book says more about the author than words and details could. The material is resonant with anyone of any age, in any time and place, whose life has opened windows into terrifying depths of the soul. Expressing this material, and sharing it, dissolved many of the old identities that traditionally appear in an "About" page. The author wishes such freedom for everyone, and yet is willing to include here some details that readers routinely seek. Thus:

Jean Ford enjoyed a career in public education as a teacher and administrator. Upon retirement, she entered a Catholic Franciscan Order for eleven years.

As a lifelong learner, she continues to study in depth the fields of psychology and spirituality, always open to explorations of the mystery of this life.
She now lives in Cottonwood, Arizona.

www.ingramcontent.com/pod-product-compliance
Lightning Source LLC
Chambersburg PA
CBHW042139290426
44110CB00002B/58